BEAUTY STRIP

BEAUTY STRIP

William Kelley Woolfitt

Texas Review Press
Huntsville, Texas

FIRST EDITION

Requests for permission to acknowledge material from the work should be
sent to:

Permissions
Texas Review Press
English Department
Sam Houston State University
Huntsville, TX 77341-2146

Cover illustration by Jeremy Miranda.

Cover design by Nancy Parsons, Graphic Design Group.

Author photograph by Rachel Schrock.

Library of Congress Cataloging-in-Publication Data

Woolfitt, William Kelley, 1974- author.

Beauty Strip / William Kelley Woolfitt. -- First edition.

pages cm

ISBN 978-1-68003-010-5 (pbk. : alk. paper)

1. Landscapes--Appalacian Region--Poetry. 2. Cities and towns--Appalacian
Region--Poetry. 3. Appalacian Region--Poetry. I. Title.

PS3623.o723B43 2014

811'.6--dc23

2014036472

For my grandparents,
Jack and Doris Kelley

Contents

III. BLUE MASON

IV. BLOOMERY

I. Dark Waters

…under the earth
there are black rooms your very body
can move through.

— Irene McKinney

Meditation on the Hands of a Boy Miner

Nails split, he cups
his hands to his chest,
hides the seams that cross

his palms, scar-lines
of labors for his father,
chunks sorted, braces built.

He clenches his hands
like tree buds—never open,
always spring. The space

inside them, so near his heart,
must be holy—formless, empty,
dark as cave streams, sump

pools, the face of the waters
where the spirit broods
before it calls out the light.

Time, the Springhouse

The burnished sun hangs on the peg of night.
Kicking my sheets, I stir the boat of my bed,

twitch when whippoorwill and peeper songs
leak through the screen, come down as a fine net

brushing my skin. Golden brown, a corona
rims the moon, egg-washed in its copper pan.

Splashes of water and light lap my walls,
crest in dream-basins, flicker

like coals mounded over ash cakes.
Rib-bones and gunnels fall, rise, fall again.

Space is the long shelf where radiance cools;
gravity, the pie safe that keeps the sweetness fresh;

time, the springhouse where phrases swim
in the dark waters of the diverted stream.

I wake with crumbs on my lips,
some gleam in the corner of my eyes.

Pea Ridge Farm, West Virginia: a Litany

Let there be forecasts from Backbone Mountain,
katydids and grasshoppers that rasp and pop up
from the mown field. If there's good hay weather,

I stay with my grandparents another day.
Let my skin be not abraded by hay stems,
timothy heads, the rough twine. Let there be aloe

for the scratch-marks on my neck, down my arms,
thin red lines. If the dim hayshed makes my nose itch
and drip, I drink ice water from a plastic jug.

If a bale rams my skinny chest, knocks me flat,
I count the motes and seeds spinning in a ray.
Let there be deer-burgers, potatoes in their jackets,

beans (half-runner), corn-on-the-cob (silver queen).
If the radio crackles like a hive, perhaps all things
are freighted, teeming, abuzz. If there are blisters

on my hands, let me see them as almost translucent.
Let there be puffballs and earthstars, stomped by boots,
sending up plumes of rich brown dust.

Ring of Earth

At sunset, I walk to the top
of the knob, zenith and center of the farm.
I take in acres my grandfather worked,
the rust-roofed sheds and pale silo, reeds
and husks; the receding pond filmed over,
in deep shadow; the lavish ironweed
willing to sprout from anything,
even bare stone. I plant my feet,

steep in the dusk. Once, I stood
with my grandfather on the knob;
he pointed his hand and named for me
four close counties. Mountains
bounded us, as if we had claimed
the middle of a fancy bowl, scalloped
and celadon-glazed. Before sickness
riddled, wasted, and thinned all that he was,

leeched the strength he gave to farming,
his work had been a strain of love. He dug
post holes, strung wire, clipped bull calves.
Once, a sinkhole opened in the meadow
where his red and whiteface cattle grazed.
Some settler a hundred years back, he said,
must have dug under us to get at the coal.
I helped fill his pickup with stones

from streambeds in the woods.
Before we dropped the stones
into the hole, he let me look.
On my hands and knees, face in a ring
of earth, I peered in and felt—
or nearly felt—a draft, a rush of breeze
that smelled like ashes and old leaves.
I took in an impossible underground room,

black and jagged, shiny and unlit.

Mountaintop Removal Site

We can't see behind the surviving trees,
the false-front hills, beauty strip
they left to hide from us the marks
of their labor, the extracted land.

For all we know, this is the same country
we've always driven through, same heaved road,
potholes, glimpse of White Oak Creek—
unless we pull over, bold as the finders
of never-seen earth, and immerse our bodies

cheaper quicker access   millions of tons

in July's green air, the liquid garble
of cicadas and towhees. And pass through
snarls of sumac, scramble up,
and haul ourselves by branches we grab
when the hill steepens,

and heed any urge that would spur us
up to the brim, where we may gaze
out at the secret place:
earth scourged and profane,
parent block, the final coal veins

450 mountains   2,400 miles of streams

torn out and trucked away, hills blasted
like shot melons, pie crust of wasted soil,
mare of the moon, the creeks stamped out,
valley fill pressed down like ancient

sediments crushing the polypous tribes.
And come closer to our own natures:
slow, willful, breath-given, dust-sized.

Downstream

After we eat the cores, the stars inside,
we go down Twelvepole Creek, skin-boat
slipping through bowers of ash, pine,
and bur oak. Fruit-fattened, we founder

downstream. We shelter beneath
our skin-boat, use sinews for fishing line.
Nothing bites. We remember how our teeth
tore into the pleasures that shined.

We eat thistles, consider what we might yet do,
given long-term soundness, the purity
of hearts that cannot be wormed through,
repossessed. May we yet find an etched tablet,

inscribed with marks for praying
the fears away, for piloting tomorrow's
handbreadth of river, its sandbars and shallows,
mudflats and meanders.

Farm Knowledge (i)

No tower brushing the underbelly
of paradise, tree-of-heaven is invasive,
modest in height, devoting its feverish
energies to the conquest of meadows,
producing seeds and the suckers

that spring forth from any root injury.
Tartarian honeysuckle, dame's rocket,
musk thistle, and autumn olive
also take hold, while the knowledge
of good and evil persists in the fragrant

panicles and hooked prickles
of multiflora rose, horn of plenty
that runs a green riot in pastures,
fields, and lots no longer tended
by tractors or scythes. Even the skilled

hunters of blackberries in June are torn
by multiflora and buckthorn, the surly
ramblers that tattoo our unwary bodies
with tiny wounds.

Firstlings

Feet still wet, mud-coated from the foaming stream,
man-with-red-eyes fetched seven quartz-studded stones,
crossed the sheep meadow, slung one stone,
and another, at man-with-blue-eyes.

Red as pokeberries, red as the carp's spiny fins,
and the stripe of his pickup, the fur of his chest,
red as the slender petals that opened in the forehead
of him-with-blue-eyes:

second-born, mother's pet, god's pretty,
who did not hunt deer, or catch fish from the stream.
He tended the ewes, took their milk and fleece,
built tumble-down fences

his sheep stepped right over. Not so heated, not so rash
blue as the veins peeking through his pale forearms,
as the hedge-flowers that he twisted around his rearview
mirror and in his straw hat,

as the gnatcatcher who nested in the hedge,
shrilled up the sun. Blood pooled on the ground
until the rain, in silvery spurts and sheets,
did what the rain will always do.

The hedge grew dense and impervious
while the birds gossiped about the weather,
did what the birds will always do.
One man fell. One man flew.

The Sinks of Gandy

*"About 1830, the wife of Thomas B. Summerfield shot an elk at
a lick near the head of Gandy Creek."*

In the woods, where ice-laden
beeches glint and drip, Anna finds
no green nubs of bittercress. No tracks,
no cone middens, no scat. To the jay
pecking into snow, she offers a pearl
of the scant lard. The jay's sharp beak
jabs her stiffening hand.

She crosses broken fence, its rails
sagging or snow-snapped. She sheds
her rough coat, lays beside her musket
in snow the color of trampled meal.
Anna could stay in this snow bed,
become a pillar of ice, freeze off
the fevery heat of the log house,
the food cries, baby spit, and sour wash.

In the blind valley below the cliffs,
the cave-mouth takes in Gandy Creek.
She dreams *she follows the creek*
as it flows underground, becomes
a dark ribbon that a body could follow
by tallow-light. At the creek's outflow,
she pours the dream-woman through,
lets her run in the next valley,

run beyond Yokum Ridge.
Near the creek, she hears a loud snort,
snow-siftings, the black cherry shaken.
A bull elk noses the cherry twigs.
First she's seen in twenty years.
She bites her cool lip. She shoots;
there is a gush of blood as he kneels,
a cloud of steam. His antler-crown

curves over her. She ties
his haunches with leg- skins, hangs them
in the cherry tree, turns for home
with her apron full of meat.

Kanawha Salt-works, 1825

Rows of stone furnaces flanked
the river they called Old Greasy.
He had vats to settle, burns

on his hands, that thumping rhythm
in his head, the steam drill's ring.
And the wheelers and jim-arounds

stacking, stomping, a separate beat.
He fixed his eyes on the ground,
tried not to see the hills cut to stubble,

gullied by rain, or the dug-out
coal-beds, their hungry gape.
The midday sky was dark as sackcloth

from the vapors, the rancid smoke.
When he gagged, the bosses called him
field-tackie, black Irish. His eyes

swimming in steam, brine for him to grain.
Pans he had to lift. Once, he dreamed
he drank cool water from a gourd

in a Mingo woman's cupped hands.
Not the river iridescent, not this crystal
rind that crackles from his skin.

May Apples

In her mirror, Ava paints herself as the old cheat's
last plaything. Her wilted celery look. She must lean
full-weight against the Dutch doors that block her in,
budge both halves with her bony knees and wrists.

From the field, she harvests may apples and bee balm,
that she might boil a cloudy tea for his sore joints,
his fireless blood. He brightens, springs from his chair,
goes out to feed his prize silver-laced Wyandotte

chickens, boasts to her about the fair, crows about
the spots and streaks of their feathers, and naps again.
From the woods, she brings thin poplar rods,
peels the bark to expose the white inner wood,

lifts his head, and hides the poplar under his pillow,
that he might be cured in his sleep. He doesn't wake,
sleeps open-mouthed. In the closet, hangers scritch
as she swats them aside. Like madcap birds, her hands

snatch and flail, yank out some sequined diaphanous
thing, and sail it around her goosepimpled body.
She interrupts his shredded wheat; he lowers his spoon.
She pleads *give me a child*; he swallows, dabs his mouth

with the plaid napkin. *I'm not God*, he says.
She keeps trying; opens pots, tubes, and tins; chooses
pale whispery stuff to powder her forehead and cheeks,
a burnt red like the poppies she planted in a tire.

And the Limberjack Dolls Shall Stomp Their Feet

At the fair, when his boot-toe taps
on plank, we move with abandon
like the spirit-stricken who shimmy
in revival. With every loose-strung joint

of our segmented bodies— poplar
torsos, chinquapin heads, limbs
of gourd-sliver—we bounce
and jar, we swing and clack.

Does he know unrest, how it bores
through our wood, laces us with tunnels
of ache and want, the heady will *to make*
that filled those who reeled

before the brass calf? While he rubs
horsehair over gut-string,
his boot plays us; we say *okay*
and then *who needs you,*

we clatter something
that's not the rhythm he asks for,
rearrange and then run away
with his beat.

Altared There in a Darksome Place

Ota Benga, a Badi pygmy from the Congo, was exhibited at the
St. Louis World's Fair and the Bronx Zoo. In 1912, the Baptist
Ministers Conference sent him to the Virginia Seminary at
Lynchburg, where he befriended the poet Anne Spencer.

In her salon, Ota Benga throttles the pencil.
Although Mrs. Spencer eases his grip,
his alphabet still buckles,
grinds down the page.

In the woods, he creeps as if weightless.
He teaches her son his deer-footed ways.
And how to greet the vibrant things
that know them as kindred,
how to thank the elms that offer them
canopy of shadow, and squirrel-chatter,
cardinal-flash.

And he shows her son the still paths
that usher them into the spruce grove,
its closet of wind.

They bring home chanterelles,
a clam fossil, a cowbird egg.

In her garden, her son learns to clean trout
from the flick of Ota Benga's wrist.
The scales they scrape rain down
on her bed of clematis and hollyhocks.
She shivers at the gleam of fish-mail
and the honed blade, his revering eyes,
her dream of ancient tongues everywhere.

II. Second Growth

The earth is full of your riches.

Psalm 104:24

Hanging Valley

Soon, the loggers will take the second-
growth Blackwater trees, drive the flying
squirrels from their woodpecker holes,

evergreen crowns, spare not one home.
Near the ruined coke ovens, the gutted
seams, I can enter the woods again,

if not for long. I sprawl beneath a hickory,
try to soak something of the forest
into my fish-belly skin. I remember what

Rukeyser said: *the first night of dreaming
was green. When the dreamers woke,
there was poetry.* If I could dream like that,

I'd stay with these woods. And declare
that I'm part-squirrel, and sprout skin-flaps,
and feast on the mast of my landing tree.

Psalm with Sheet-web Spiders as Temple Singers

My words cannot express, but oh let me try
to tell you how free and how newly alive
I felt, hiking today (first time since July)
in mid-September. I meant to head
for Pickle Branch, the Dragon's Tooth,
but started out from the wrong trailhead.
Sheet-web spiders had hung out their banners.
I found more speech pouring from fragments
of sunlight on the ground, from the lichens,
rotting limbs in the leaf litter, and stones
shattered and upheaved. Nature had its own
tongue, the inanimate world a liveliness,
and oh I was free, awake, inside out,
a filament, a breeze, a whisper,
while I crossed Sawtooth Ridge; I wore
swaths of blessing where the skin should be.

The Blight Trees

after "O Taste and See" by Denise Levertov

The world is with me, in cornea, cochlea, on tongue,
fingertips, within throat and ribs, in powers
and quantities I cannot guess. Like overripe fruit,
I cling to the branch, doze, yawn, fork and bite
a half-iced TV dinner, stare at the tube long enough
to know stupor. But sometimes, the sleeping flowers

yield to sun, rain, Miracle Gro, and are transformed.
Like a defibrillated pacemaker, the risen dead. One bite
of peach pie that my grandmother baked, the fruit
from blight trees staked in her yard, is enough
to jumpstart me—or the snowflake, that thrill to tongue
and brain. What frosty savor, what multiform

design. My tongue has power enough to reform
or demolish; the earth is fruit for me when I take a bite.

Blackwater Gorge

Peripheries, I say,
convincing myself, as I follow trails
carved from the scars of a branch line's
rail beds. *Where the world hoards its riches,*
creatures, packets of motion and heat.

I clamber into sphagnum bogs, find
no reason to believe. I denounce
the man with condo dreams, estimated
feet of red spruce and yellow birch
firing through his veins. I lift stone slabs,

plead, am patient as a stump.
The gorge seals its moist cavities,
will not show the salamanders, slippery
and brass-flecked, said to breathe oxygen
through their marvelous skins.

House with Two Doors

i.

Bottom door writes down license plates.
With a brass monkey paw for a knocker
and its shadeless window face-sized,
bottom door staves off the sloping yard,
vine-throttled hills, power line buzz,
frackers' drone, and wings that rustle
like old bank notes. Bottom door holds
and will not spill the interior rooms,
periwinkle and dust-moted, the chests,
wardrobes, the preacher's typewriter
unwieldy as a smithy's forge,
firedogs, old mail drifting over counters,
and on the stove a kind of potato soup,
perpetually simmering. Add half-and-half
this evening, or bacon drippings,
a clump of ramps tomorrow, if Ava refuses
the bread of idleness and goes out
through the bottom door,
ambles the deforested scrub-woods
and remembers the spade.

ii.

Upper door squelches loose talk
that would seep out. Upper door,
tight-lipped juror, hushes the second-story hall,
its cobwebs and lint, its paint in lizard-scales.
Given the cheep of hope pecking its shell,
Ava would pry up the nails, stand within
the balcony's iron petals till the road offered
some gladsome sound: the maracas of gravel
churned under wheels, a soft hum,
the brush of dead ash leaves.
Storms felled that tree, unmoored the house,
left the upper door groaning and askew;
hired hands stripped the balcony,
tamped the foundation down.
Take the vinyl poncho, cash for the merchant,
or trade the walnuts and pawpaws.
May nothing touch her, if she walks the ditch
or braves the shoulder to town,
if the sun shorts out,
if the sky pledges rain.

In the Reformatory, Billie Holiday Refuses to Sing

1947: Federal Woman's Reformatory at Alderson, West Virginia

Her fans send heaps of letters and cards.
She would toss all that mail into the air,
make a vanity of wind, a blizzard
in her room. But the guards send back

any envelope not from immediate family,
and hers are dead. And they rifle through
her packages, keep the pears, and lacy
gowns, and gin in rhinestone flasks.

She scans the lady warden's flyer.
Talent night, good fun for all.
She doesn't give a damn about
the amateur show, refuses to sing

about juke joints, a rotten lover
who wastes his paycheck, black bodies
hanging like scuppernongs.
She insists she's here for punishment,

for tomato worms and weeds,
the pig parlor, the kitchen sink,
these toilsome nights they lock her
in the cottage, lonely and foul as a tomb.

While she serves, it's her time to refrain.
Her feelings and her voice are a queen's
best jewels and muskrat furs
saved in mothballs, packed away.

The Eyes of Doves

after Frank Buchser's Black Girl in a Stream
oil on canvas

1867

Away from Washington city, she runs
    away from stenography, she runs
away with him, she runs. From train cinders,
    from village racket, tobacco farms,

through the rhododendron tunnel,
    through its leafy chambers of cool and heat,
with the Swiss man stumbling after, she runs
    to Laurel Creek, the secluded banks

she thought of. Beneath pine rafters,
    beneath cedar beams, he glances;
in a grove for two, he makes sure
    they are alone, then unwraps his easel.

In this year of despisals, she laughs,
    slips off her shoes, stockings, blue
tarlatan dress, slips off her camisole,
    petticoat, and trembles before him.

He holds back,
    afraid she'll vanish, a bubble of froth
melting in the air, if he chances
    the littlest touch.

She wades in, and twists her body
    contrapposto, and stands ankle-deep
in languors, in dapples where shadows lap
    over the grottos of her skin.

She mouths a word
    for him to read as he mixes green
for locust leaves, and umber
    for shagbark and hush.

Pulp Town

i.

Old trees topple; laundry hung on lines
snags the mill's reek of rotten cabbage;
log trucks bust up the roads. Screen doors clatter.
Houses fill with smoke. A boy and a girl
steal the kitchen money, the church wine,
take turns driving a truck too fast, shoot rabbits,
bring to the taxidermist any scrap of furry luck
flashing through their unburnt lives.

ii.

People size up the new neighbors. Father, twitchy,
bug-eyed, too nervous to speak to the mailman;
outspoken mother with frizzy hair, won't tie up
her day-glories, teaches her children Portuguese.
Come summer, they pitch a tent in their front yard,
a haven for dandelions and stickseed.
Unclean murmurs circle around them,
buzz the edge of sleep.

Muriel Rukeyser in West Virginia

Fayetteville, 1936

Muriel meets the driller's wife
at the diner. She tells Muriel,
"Try the spice cake."

Muriel's notepad unnerves her.
She peers into her coffee,
frets her colorless dress.

Scratching paper, Muriel tries to find words
for her thin hand, raveled sweater.

Muriel scribbles *diverted river, emptied bed,
stagnant puddles*, the five mile section
the townspeople call *the dries.*

The wife says paper deceives,
she trusts word-of-mouth,
the Lord of hosts hovering overhead.

She knew the tunnel for what it was.
Her man said no choice. He wouldn't budge.

Scribble *dry drill, dynamite, silica, stone.*

When he coughs in the night,
she has to turn him;
the bed rattles, their babies wake.

When he dresses in the morning,
she sees bruises where her fingers
pressed him, dark blues, little plums.

Successional

I cocoon myself in the dome tent,
sputtering and spent, no longer in a rush.
The pond a disk of indigo glass, the moon
thinner than the spines of black locust twigs
frosted at the pasture's edge, the chink in the ice,
the dim glow of the expiring flashlight.

My works do not wake. When I plead
with the silent dark, snow comes down thick
as kettle-boiled apple butter, sure to stick to sassafras,
sumac, and chrome letters on the spare-parts
flatbed truck. Infertile eggs turn to pellets
in the ooze of puddles lidded with ice.

The down sack warms my clammy skin.
I dream of grass stems, bread crumbs,
a tangle of hawthorns beaded with dew
and laced with webs. The world hums beneath
its rind of snow. I hear dogwood branches shake;
then the piping of a bird; then silence;

then something, the sunless murmur
at the cusp of day.

The Visions of Bessie Harvey

From 1977 until her retirement in 1983, the vernacular artist
Bessie Harvey worked as a housekeeper's aide in a hospital,
where she gave dolls to the patients. She was the mother of
eleven children. She and her second husband lived in Alcoa,
Tennessee, a factory town in the foothills of the Smoky
Mountains.

i.

Pick up that stick.

She finishes the healing-dolls, brings their spirits out.
She takes them to a woman with holes in her lungs.
To a cankered man who smells like burnt soup.
To a woman still and cool as stone. She lingers
at each bed, sings to all that aching flesh.

After she feeds her husband and kids, tidies the kitchen,
she slips away to the woods. Her son drinks too much,
fights too much, laughs at the threat of jail.
She rests her cheek against tree bark, watches
fuzzy clouds stream through the alder limbs.

She lifts a branch from the ground, learns it by hand.

> Gnarls.
> Grooves.
> Two burls the shape of eyes.

The paint she dabs on the branch
wakes the likeness already there:
boy-doll with twisted legs, crooked back,
his asymmetrical head like a potato
sprouting baby potatoes.

He isn't hers. The sick folks need him more.

ii.

Time eats the wood into shapes.

For by sawyer, borer, carpenter worm, bark beetle,
by rot and years that weather, all the dolls
and stump-pieces were created.

The trees speak to her of their maker.

She takes up roots, limbs, pieces of stump.
With beads, cowry shells, feathers, putty, penny nails,
duct tape, human hair, marbles, fingernail varnish,
she makes visible all the fullness that dwells in them.
So that she can have somebody to talk to.
So that she won't be afraid.

The dolls, she names Eve, and Jezebel,
and Queen of Sheba. Moses, Snake Woman,
Prehistoric Bird. Black Horse of Revelations.
King of Africa. Two Heads Better Than One.

And the stump-pieces, these she names Kingdom Seat.
Slaughter of the Innocents. The World.

iii.

It's a type of ministry in this wood.

Strangers pay good cash, crowd her yard
to view the likenings whose sap-blood she rouses.
Not her neighbors. They snub her, call her
voodoo woman, backbite, don't stop by.

When she tries to quilt for the church sale,
she has to yank the stitches, start again.
She tries different fits, but can't proceed
by pattern, or by feel.

Her oven overheats like a thing possessed,
ruins her apple pie, chars it like a sin.

For all of it, she blames the dolls. Moves them
from her workshop in the basement
to the trash heap out back. Drizzling the mess
with kerosene, she groans at her husband
to bring matches. And lye soap, to cure her skin.

iv.

All the roots are little people.

Sick in bed, she tells herself she should get up,
fuss over her husband and kids, join the choir,
help with Sunday school crafts.

He coaxes her to go walking by the lake
where he likes to fish. She clasps his arm,
looks away from sticks scattered along the shore.
She sees pairs of eyes, possible faces, doll-bodies,
in their front door, and church pews,
and mixing spoons. And circle-designs
in the stovepipe. And seahorses in the whorls
and wood-grains of certain boards.

Her kids tiptoe, treat her like a bauble of glass.

She reads of Ezekiel, who saw the whirlwind
from the north, fire enfolding itself and bright as amber,
a creature with four faces, and wings, and calf's feet.
People said he was crazed by his vision, his gift.

She slips away to the woods. She lifts to her ear
an old branch, knobby and lichened, fallen
from a crab apple tree. She hears it hum,
and then she heeds the buzz in her hands.

III. Blue Mason

...revise the psalm
if that should frighten you: sew up belief
if that should tear...

—Gwendolyn Brooks

Acolyte at the Bell Stand inSt. Anne's Churchyard

When he tugs the rope, the bell creaks.
Flakes of rust tumble down, cobwebs
catch in his hair, and the empty nests
of swallows unravel, pelt the ground

with dirt-gobs and faded stems.
As he stoops to sift the nest shreds,
his hand branches, tells
of the rasp and whir in his blood

to quackgrass and chervil that spring
out of the dirt when light pours
from the tipped crock of sky.
When he yanks the rope again,

the air splits; the bell pitches
back and forth, his bones ring,
and notes spill from the bell
said to have lost its tongue.

Bystander at the Immaculate Conception

after Charles Umlauf's War Mother
sculpture, cast stone

1939

Moss-barnacles speckle her stone body,
the way particles of darkness and bright
bunch like fruit-flies over her brow,
her nostrils, fill her with the wish to bear
the favor, the sundering cries, the child

she'll be pressed to lay upon this bloodied
altar or the next. I kneel at her feet. I believe
the flies have landed. I hold out my hands
to refuse, I delay the victim I should lift
from my own daily rubble. I decline

legs bent like reeds, fingers fear-fused, a face
hollow and animal, the mews of a singed
fledgling, a shelled bird. Meanwhile,
she's flushed, incandescent, metamorphic.
She's shaded through. If I had to cradle

and then lay down, I believe first I'd hold
myself dumb and cold as a slab, then lock
my arms, make them rigid, a steady shelf;
maybe then I could let some unknowable
pass in and out of my body of stone.

To Toil Not

Even on these nights of swelter,
when brine glazes our listless skins,
the gleaners pour out from the cool
recesses of Stillhouse Cave and comb the edge
habitats of karst country, where groundwater's

drippy metronome nibbles out maternity
caves and bachelor roosts. The bats must want,
as everyone does, to toil not, to open
their mouths in ardor, to shake off
liquid calcite, ceiling-spittle,

and fly like scarves of parchment
flung by some juggler's fraught hands,
and at the feeding grounds, to pack on fat
for the coming winter, tuck with gusto
into the hayfield's larder of moths.

Penny, Fossil, Button-shank, Milk Tooth

The three of us had been
a life raft, but last year
we busted up for good,
fare-thee-well, milkweed pods,
let the hoarse old wind take us
where it will. There's no time
capsule any of us would line
with mementoes and scraps
to unearth in a hundred years.
Groundwater trickles down
our dripstone bodies,
grooves the zagging trough
of the Lobelia Saltpeter Cave.
Our toes could be taken
for alabaster, carved
into flasks like those the sinner
women filled with perfume,
and carried to the home
of Simon the Leper to pour
over the rabbi for the Feast
of Unleavened Bread.
Something crumbles below us,
wizened and thinning, tucked
under, wrapped in,
Indian or wheat-stalk penny,
clam fossil, dragoon's brass
button-shank, damned tooth,
blue mason of air.

The Wisdom of Peaches

In his journey he is gone; he may have
sent us peaches for such a time as this.

He knew how to give good gifts.
At summer's end, we stand in a ring

around the tree in smoky-blue evening.
The tallest among us brandishes a rake,

claws peaches from the top branches
as we scatter and duck. The peaches say

live without parachutes,
for sailing down with a billow of silk

only dulls the brain, steals freedom
from falling, slows the future

that still must be. We bury
our faces in fruit-flesh and sunset fur,

crimson and gold and juices all over
fingers and chins. We shall not want,

for we have peaches to eat.
We check the groundfalls for bruises

and decay, sing the song of plummet
that the peaches sing as they long

for solid ground, for beds in the grass,
and leap from the tree.

Snakebit

The preacher's house another cast-off,
stuffed with ratty sofas, stacks of cord-bound
gospel tracts, rolls of tent canvas
and coiled guy-lines that barricade
the upstairs hall. Cardboard and blanket
squares taped to windows. Ava putters

from room to room, cuts his suits for a quilt,
passes his guitar to the garbage-man, burns
his sermons and balsa planes. Better to eat
cleaning-lye than to foul her mouth with the false
speech that pleased him, better to touch a rattler
than him who switched her, made her repent.

Each day she patches more holes,
casts out the chill, peels some green
from the wad of ones, mails the stepson.
She nurses the sick aloe, boils bones
for carcass soup, feeds the tongues
of gold fire in the woodstove.

Interior Detail, 1938

after Walker Evans' Interior Detail,
West Virginia Coal Miner's House

gelatin silver print

In Evans' photograph, the walls hold up
just barely, hold out some of the panting
wind that seeks to overwhelm, hisses like
a punctured lung, discharges a low moan, coughs
dust against the walls, pounds new tempos,

does not soothe. The improvisations of poverty
expand, persist, repeat. What miner's woman
would not dribble a measure of kerosene
into the syrup bottle, twist and set aflame
the rag-wick, and diligently seek the silver

needle that fell from her pincushion,
so that she might hem the piece-goods
she cut from the butterfly pattern?
The finder can eke out a life here, lash
a rocker from willow limbs, supple

and long, her genius and industry patchworking
the walls from scrap wood, tinplate, cardboard,
drug store and soft drink ads, more of the same
to rig the baggy ceiling. Her broom rests upright,
her swept floor clean as a picked bone.

Sparrow Lament

You fall, sparrow egg, God-eyed leaf,
black grit of coal, kernel of wheat,
gold blown from the stalk. You lift wood,
trudge, and lurch, your back pulped. You would
spit up the cup-dregs for relief—

but no, you want not; you believe
your master's dream. You toss your dreams
like chaff to the breeze. You lift wood.

You fall,

    thin coin,

       widow's all,

          copper seed

into the mouth of the box. She
brushed you a hundred times, so good
to hold, but better to drop. Wood
weights you, snapped bone, windblown leaf.

You fall.

Our Lady of the Mills

Dodge the filthy clumps,
their chilblained faces,
rabbit eyes, broken teeth.
Ease into the stone
church, the one work
you will give them: the virgin,
charcoal-lined, comfort
for the people in their hours
at the furnace, the spools.

With paregoric and tonic bitters,
endure the stained light,
cold arches, and eye sockets.
Empty, unpainted, the dreadful
ovals will tell what she felt
when she touched her son,
cool and rigid as marble
awaiting the chisel, pale
as old muslin, spilt cream.

Water Shrew as the Apostle Peter

The water shrew finds jetsam in his feeding pool
and larva-sized nubs of shattered glass
in the leaf mold. On the lip of the creek,

an old tin can that the shrew nudges
with his whiskery nose, that he frees
from the sedges and live-forever weeds.

Rusted to razor-lace, fine as a riffleshell,
the can holds little of the creek,
its indelible minerals, smorgasbord of debris.

What it holds—decaying vegetation,
a little silt—spills when the shrew jostles it.
Crepuscular in his habits, lissome

in his body when he dives
for the flatworm that he may
or may not find. Sheathed in air bubbles,

the shrew rises from the region of muck,
the compromised waters, and eyes the can
as it drifts, as the current has its way with it,

fragile craft. When caddisflies brush
the waters of his pool, the shrew catches
bubbles in his toe hairs—picture

pearly slippers, two pairs—then runs
the creek's surface, zags across the sheen.

Home Remedies

Hang pie pans and ribbons of foil
to scare the deer.

Choose a new shirt, his slacks,
and bus-driving shoes for him
to wear in the earth.

Squirt dish soap on beefsteak
and big boy leaves.

Stand by the long box, say
he looks good in that shade of blue.

Try hot sauce when the soap fails.

Nod when a relative says *he's not
really here,* meaning only the spirit
has ceaseless life.

Crumble soil with swollen fingers.

Tell the relative, *yes, but I love
what's still here.*

Tie drier sheets to the stakes.

Listen to his song tapes, put pictures
on the mantle.

Wish for a bag of hair.

Farm Knowledge (ii)

We are the branches. In the vine we abide.
I think I better understand words like these
when I recall his half-runner and pole beans
that looped and twined around the stakes

he lashed together in teepee frames.
Those scraggly green tendrils
would climb anything,
braid around each other like helix chains,

hogtie the bean pods so tightly
that when picking beans,
he had to break the vines. Now he is gone,
but his life is in me.

Rain is in the blossom, sun is in the seed.
The times of together and without
blur at steam-train-speed. The word *tree*
fills the cells of the clingstone peaches

we eat, the earth soaks the farmer's-
market-vegetables we stir-fry in sesame oil.
Part of you stays with me sprouts
through the rotten log of *good-bye.*

Pentecost with Yellowthroats and Ovenbirds

In the uncertain days, in early spring, while the outer world
  throbs with pear bloom, green bud, and frog eggs
  that glisten in the saturated muck, while the rooms inside

our small stone house fill with ice breath, gray ash,
  I rummage through nursery catalogs, tear out
  calla bulb and gourd seed I could order, then kindle

those glossy pages on the hearth-slab, that unarable bed.
  In the barely-speaking days, in the not-touching,
  the smoky flannels, the cease-to-be, I rub the window

again, and again pick threads from the curtain, and cool
  my brow against the small bubbled panes. I shun
  my studio, creep down to the basement

where you watercolor scene after scene of our house
  in the winter just past. Feverish, your work,
  your not-answering. You mumble if I say *I heated*

some food, if I stare over your shoulder at our tiny house,
  the waves of snow, the gouache you layer
  and layer on, skipping meals, and bed, communion

of mouth on ear, body twining around body for warmth.
  The one oblivious, the other letting the one be.
  I retreat to the window again, its brittle chill of glass.

Two warblers, April's arrivals, land on the toolshed,
  descend and search the length of a fallen spruce.
  The first gathers materials—for a hooded nest

in the glade, I think—rootlet, hair, sepal of trout lily,
  some fine thing to line the inner chamber
  of the nest. The second crams its beak with grubs.

Either could be an earth-sign, something I should read
    before I pad downstairs, enter that cavernous room,
    and try to cross the spaces cloven between us,

to speak to you the first word,
    that small green kernel,
    in a language your own.

IV. Bloomery

...mist hangs in thin layers...
like rotting snow-ice sucked away
almost to spirit...

— Elizabeth Bishop

Credo at Raccoon Branch on the Appalachian Trail

At 29, I moved to snow country. I should have feared
the meager air that frosts eyebrows and breaths,
the flattery, the rationed invitation. My life
dwindled in the room of drafts

and scribbled pages. If I spoke,
it was to admire freeze-frame. If I ate,
it was to chew splinter match. I made much
of drifted blanks and low blue flame.

I kept refusing dry mouth and flakes of skin;
I called my hands good, and they were good.
I pushed the bar from my chest, I learned
frog stand and cow asana; in the aquamarine room,

I stood beneath waters that washed me clean.
From my palms, I scoured calluses and ink stains.
I hid cohosh sprigs in my pillowcase; I fastened
my eyes on the hanging blinds, on cube of moon

and slatted sky. Beneath the Jacob's ladder quilt,
I dreamed *I was stepping toward the sun,*
its coal-heart like the door inside the iris of the eye,
walking north with spring along a blazed path,

with a pebble in my hand and a new name that I spoke
to colt's foot, trillium, and cucumber-root.
That name bubbles out of me, I can't stop repeating it
but I don't want to scare it away,

so I let myself breathe it. To my knapsack,
mess kit, and bandana, I breathe it,
and to each turkey tail and bracket fungi
that girdles hump of stone, shank of tree.

Absentee

I come from the careening wrong turn, Holy Rollers,
Queen Anne's lace, and fists;

siltstone and slate embossed with ferns; bituminous coal
that pocks our land with holes

and pits, makes an overseas company rich.
My trailer stands

at the end of a flood-prone road I never would have found.
Showers at night fill my gutters

with knuckles of hail, scattershot ice a bruising
reminder to me

that I am really in my body, and not in a dream,
when I go out to smell

the world set alive. Taking welts on my back,
I move past wood scraps

and junk cars to Buffalo Creek, where I fill my jug
with the true, the dark, the raw,

a speaking-forth of sulfur ooze.

Note to Slash Fires, to Draglines

There are forces in this world, principalities and powers, that wrench away the things that are loved, people and land, and return only exile.

Denise Giardina

My tongue is brass. My feet are brass.
I have not love, not prophecy.
I am no angel, no spyglass.
I trudge outside, peer through the haze
of slash fires for any little task
to keep me alive. I polish
the vessels and horns
of the entertainment center,
make them shine.

My hills are slag. My mountains are slag.
Leveled by draglines a hundred feet high,
dynamite, ravenous trucks.
I let them clearcut, flatten.
Dig every chunk. Reap every stone.
I fill my cart with bargains,
jumbo packs. It is so easy
to shut my eyes, not speak.

My scissors are rust. My tacks are rust.
For news of the candidates' debates,
I comb the web, print out her reproof:
If the Statue of Liberty was here,
you'd tear it up for scrap metal.
I clip and pin paper to cork, prick
the skin of my thumb and lose
not one drop of blood.

My horizon is tin. My sky is tin.
Unending plane, flat and wide and gray,
forged to be all-encompassing, a lid
sealed with gloom. No hole
to leak in the sun. I freeze when I sleep,
dream that I'm scrambling up a ladder,
I forgot to bring camera, blowtorch,
all I have is the nail between my teeth.

Antiphon for the Office of the Dead

a powder box and swans-down puff
her limp stocking, a green satin fan
spangled with dragonflies, curling tongs
small muslin bags, a pumice stone

bits of skin, cut-glass bottles, cuticle
knife, a darner, nail powder, sealing wax
spirals of his hair, glove buttoner
orangewood stick, gauze balls, shoe lift

velvet brush, rabbit's foot, pots of rouge
lip salve, cold cream plumbed by her
tired fingers, silver trays of hatpins
hairpins, safety pins, to hold, to prick

foxtail scarf with chain, scrimshaw
manicure box with sweet pea vines
carved in the whale-bone lid, hand-mirror
holding his breath, a smudged cloud

Inside the Boarded-Up Slaughterhouse

I slip into the killing room like raw silk,
a petal of smoke. My arms are feelers
waving in the dark. My nose and pores
glean messages borne on the laden air:
blood stored up, offal, fats. Bones from
creatures obedient to us, saved to make
handles, crucifixes, rosaries, cameos.
Eyes squinched, I can still map *oil house*
and *hide cellar* inside my eyelids, trace
coagulation vat in bright spidery lines.

When He Sings

Her sister predicts, *if you go*
to cadet nursing school, you'll do
the same as all those girls: fall for

a farmer from Lost Creek, drop out
if he tells you to. Think of slow waters,
dragonflies, matted leaves,

swirls of scum. Think of his hands,
smeared with pine sap, grease, ash,
the fluids of small animals he skins,

pelts of muskrat and skunk
he stretches, nails to planks.
He brings his guitar to the alley

behind her boardinghouse, mimics
Ernest Tubb, the Texas Troubadour,
sings "Walking the Floor Over You."

She hates country and Western;
she slams the window. Too late.
His song flaps around her room,

spreads through her like the black
coffee that heats chilled blood.
Her sister advises, *if you marry*

in the evening, don't wear white.
A better choice is navy blue.
She sees his hands cracked in winter,

the record player he'll buy them,
apples bending the limbs,
signs and predictions come true.

Darkly

Killdeer is a shorebird, a wader,
carrier of pebbles and wood chips
to the ground-nest that holds the eggs
he saves with his limp wing trick
and nail-sharp scream. Every spring,
he returns to the green-gold hills.
Ditch brink his improvised home.
At night, killdeer sees an ocean darkly,
refracted in dreams, eddy or trickle,
ditch-water threading his sleep.

*

Checking for mail, near the ditch,
the woman hears killdeer's cry. She is wick,
she is taper, the call in spring,
the chorus frog, the wait before
following the notes of her beloved
into that open country
without barbed wire or multiflora rose.
Some glimmer spills down,
her dream of how that unknowable,
undreamable will be.

The Bird Collector

While others are immersed in deep schemes, in building towns
and purchasing plantations, I am entranced in contemplation
over the plumage of a lark, or gazing like a despairing lover on
the lineaments of an owl.

Alexander Wilson, 1810

[The Shawnee] are a People of no Settlement but rambling from
Place to Place.

Tasattee, 1752

The water is the same as yesterday's, as far as he can see.
On a shooting trip, Wilson steers his skiff between banks
that could be the same wooded banks that rose up yesterday.
No pintails, no purple grackles, no sand martins.
No horn blares from a Kentucky boat. No sugar camp
coughs up rags of smoke in the close foothills. No cries
of big-horned owls jar his dreams. Only the Ohio River
for him to ponder, its water the same, the same, the same.
Bewildering. Streaming, streaming, streaming
like the lines of his life — rifle barrel, skiff's planes,
his body when he floats on his back. When he sights
down his torso, through his toes. All his lines
recede, recede, recede, he's a vanishing point,
an eggshell spot   a vapor   a bubble of spit

*

The water the same. Yesterdays as far as he can see.
Solitary, unfrequented, alone, river for a friend,
for an enemy. No human to speak to, no bird
to ponder, none since the storm assailed him.
Slap of waves, crash of trees, he cried out, only the river
answered, only the wind, and he fought the river,
fought his skiff, and flung himself ashore.
Fisher-people carried him into a hut
made of saplings and clay. Frozen mouths, wary eyes.

The men peeled his sopping clothes, took his pistols,
his powder flask, covered him with robes of fur.
The women gave him corn mush, a coin of black sugar,
a lump of pickled fish. On their sleeping platform,
he dreamed among them. One snored, one whispered,
one blew notes from a bundle of reeds.

*

the water   the yesterdays far   he can see
when he laps the Ohio from his bailer and swallows fast.
Dunks his head, or dives down. When he tries to wash,
to purify, to stave off. Here's the giant paddlefish head
he's saved for Peale's Museum in Philadelphia.
Pottery shreds he numbers. Conch beads he bought
from a farmer whose hogs ranged over an Indian grave
sixty feet high. In his strongbox, the scalpel, white thread.
The bird-skins whose feathers he dresses with his fingers,
re-sets and re-smoothes.

King's Creek Nocturne

With hands of mahogany, hands
of amber and muscovado sugar,

catch the moonlight that spills
into the room, stipples the highboy,

your counterpanes. Dream of stretched
vellum instead of your ledger, the iron-

master portraited or in the flesh, wire
scratches in primer-white. His back pearls

when you wash it. Trace the muscles
that lift whipsaw and broad-axe.

By day, keep his numbers, bid them stand
in tidy rows: skillets, hollow-ware;

cannonballs, cords of wood burnt
to charcoal, then shoveled into the mouth

of the bloomery that shadows acres of slash
along the creek. While orange embers

hiss in the grate, find nonsense
in his equations, misappraisals, pencil slips.

Your work I require means *fond of.*
Shoulder, freckled and bare, your hands

means *with him, a life.* Sum up the pounds
of charcoal; the petals of sponge iron;

stumps of walnut, maple, and beech.

Cyanotype, 1880

after *Thomas Anshutz's* Boys with a Boat, Ohio
River, Near Wheeling, West Virginia

*cyanotype — bluish photograph obtained by
sensitizing paper with cyanide*

Soon, millwork will melt them down,
reshape their muscles, soot their faces

as they dodge cranes, slam furnace doors,
shear cooled iron into squares. Today, these boys

skip the spelling bee, the snarls of arithmetic,
teacher's darting eye. Anshutz pays them bits

of licorice to pose for a tableau of boys at play.
They strip, drag the boat into the water, stand

spraddle-legged, face the far shore, the mill
that rumbles, spews grit. The cyanotype blues

the boys' bony shoulder-blades and knobby spines,
blues the pinched sky and ash-clotted river;

the everywhere-smoke blurs the trees,
smudges the boy-bodies, and fuzzes the air.

Flat-Spired Three-Toothed Snail

Dog days, shut sky, zero rain,
wood sorrel and lamb's tongue
smell like hot pennies,
copper scorch. Tiny blazes almost
kindle in the leaf litter, almost
give off sputters of smoke.

Three-tooth struggles, sheds
his faith in the surety of rain—
for he has sensed warnings
in his several horns (which serve
as his noses, also his eyes),
has felt in his soft parts

pangs of dryness,
the pestilence that mortifies flesh.
He slips into the upheaved rock,
basilica of gritstone, its aperture
scarcely bigger than his own.
He passes through the vestry,

descends to the fissure-nave,
its font of moisture a sign to him
something like the unbidden tears
of our own carved saints, rivulet
of life flowing from stone. Didn't
the poet say to drink whatever juices

we can squeeze from the earth?
Three-tooth secretes his shell, shapes
its apex and spire-whorls, patches
the temple that houses him,
mixes his mortar from calcium
in the dark soil that he eats.

Boy with Kite

Thirteen years old and bundled
against the chill, he pastes rags and papers
to a frame that's cockeyed, loose,
all droop and strange angles.

What the kite needs is a breeze to rise.
Sticks poking out, paper ripping,
it catches the smallest blown breath
like a dead leaf taking to flame,

and swings from his hands, swoops and glides.
He runs forward, unreels the spool. Someday,
he will go out, and instead of this wind
so cold it might be from heaven's iced dome,

he believes there will be a girl, freckled,
brunette, quick eyes and feet, warm as the blue
mittens on his hands, glad to run
alongside him, to fling puffball dust

at him in the ironweed fields,
and curl against him as he sleeps.
If he goes on running, it will
take him to a joy that breaks him.

He reels in the wind-torn kite
before it lifts him from his skin.

Acknowledgments

I would like to thank the editors of the following periodicals, in which many of these poems appeared, sometimes in earlier versions.

ABZ: "Snakebit"
Apalachee Review: "Boy with Kite"
Blueline : "Psalm with Sheet-web Spiders as Temple Singers"
Cave Wall: "Acolyte at the Bell-stand in St. Anne's Churchyard"
Christianity & Literature: "Sparrow Lament"
Connotation Press: "In the Reformatory, Billie Holiday Refuses to Sing"
The Cossack Review: "Credo at Raccoon Branch on the Appalachian Trail"
drafthorse: "Cyanotype, 1880," "Firstlings," "The Eyes of Doves"
Four Way Review: "Antiphon for the Office of the Dead"
Free State Review: "Bystander at the Immaculate Conception"
Gulf Coast: "Altared There in a Darksome Place"
Hayden's Ferry Review: "Interior Detail, 1938," "Penny, Fossil, Button-shank, Milk Tooth"
Indiana Review: "Home Remedies," "When He Sings," "Ring of Earth," "Successional," "Pea Ridge Farm, West Virginia: a Litany"
ISLE: Interdisciplinary Studies in Literature and Environment: "Farm Knowledge (i)"
Kestrel: "Darkly"
The Ledge: "The Wisdom of Peaches"
Mid-American Review: "The Visions of Bessie Harvey"
Motif: "Muriel Rukeyser in West Virginia"
Natural Bridge: "Note to Slash Fires, to Draglines"
North American Review: "Mountaintop Removal Site"
Notre Dame Review: "Inside the Boarded-up Slaughterhouse"
Now and Then: the Appalachian Magazine: "Kanawha Salt-works, 1825"
Ottawa Arts Review: "Pentecost with Yellowthroats and Oven birds"
Passages North: "Pulp Town"

Poetry International: "Farm Knowledge (ii)"
Prime Number: "And the Limberjack-Dolls Shall Stomp Their Feet"
Quarterly West: "Time, the Springhouse"
Radar Poetry: "Our Lady of the Mills"
Rock & Sling: "Downstream"
r.k.v.r.y: "Absentee"
Sakura Review: "House with Two Doors"
Shenandoah: "The Blight Trees"
Southern Humanities Review: "May Apples"
Still: the Journal: "The Bird Collector"
Talking Leaves: "Absentee"
Threepenny Review: "Flat-Spired Three-Toothed Snail"
Tiger's Eye: "Meditation on the Hands of a Boy Miner"
Town Creek Poetry: "King's Creek Nocturne," "Water Shrew as the Apostle Peter"
Virginia Quarterly Review Instapoetry Series: "Muriel Rukeyser in West Virginia"

I am grateful for the editors and publishers of the chapbooks in which several of these poems previously appeared: *The Salvager's Arts* (Seven Kitchens Press, 2013), *Chorus Frog* (Yellow Flag Press, 2014), and *The Boy with Fire in His Mouth* (Epiphany Editions, 2014).

I also wish to thank the following individuals whose encouragement, wisdom, and generosity made this book possible: all my teachers, especially Robin Becker, Todd Davis, Charlotte Holmes, Julia Spicher Kasdorf, Linda Furgerson Selzer, Gerry LaFemina, Cathryn Hankla, Inman Majors, Mary Dillow Stewart, Barbara Rasmussen, Joanne Van Horn, and Martin Lammon; my friends; my family; and Sara, truest of companions—we are making a run.

Notes

"Mountaintop Removal Site" borrows language from Shirley Stewart Burns' "Mountaintop Removal in Central Appalachia," Marianne Moore's "To a Steam Roller," and Frances E. W. Harper's "Christianity."

"Kanawha Salt-works, 1825" is informed by John E. Stealey's *The Antebellum Kanawha Salt Business and Western Markets*, Mary Lee Settle's *Know Nothing*, and Anne Newport Royall's *Sketches of History, Life, and Manners in the United States.*

"Altared There in a Darksome Place" borrows its title and some language from several poems by Anne Spencer, including "Lady, Lady."

The italicized lines in the fourth stanza of "Hanging Valley" paraphrase Muriel Rukeyser's poem "The Sixth Night: Waking."

"Muriel Rukeyser in West Virginia" is a fictional account of Rukeyser's 1936 trip to Gauley Bridge to investigate the Hawks Nest tunnel disaster. It responds to Jake Adam York's "Walt Whitman in Alabama."

"The Visions of Bessie Harvey" uses several phrases adapted from interviews and statements given by Harvey.

"Credo at Raccoon Branch on the Appalachian Trail" is after Irene McKinney's "At 24."

"Absentee" takes its title from Barbara Rasmussen's *Absentee Landowning and Exploitation in West Virginia, 1760-1920.*

"Flat-Spired Three-Toothed Snail" is after Elizabeth Bishop's "Giant Snail."